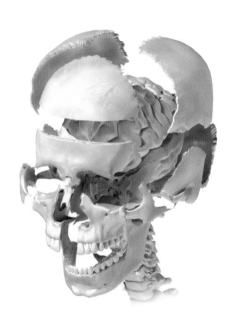

Published in 2014 by The Rosen Publishing Group, Inc.
29 East 21st Street, New York, NY 10010

Credits and acknowledgments
KEY tr=top right; c=center; bl=bottom left; bg=background

GI = Getty Images; iS = istockphoto.com; TF = Topfoto; TPL = photolibrary.com

front cover bg iS; **18**tr GI; **20**bl TPL; **28**tr GI; c TPL; **28–29**bg iS; c TF; **30–31**bg iS

All illustrations copyright Weldon Owen Pty Ltd

Weldon Owen Pty Ltd
Managing Director: Kay Scarlett
Creative Director: Sue Burk
Publisher: Helen Bateman
Senior Vice President, International Sales: Stuart Laurence
Vice President Sales North America: Ellen Towell
Administration Manager, International Sales: Kristine Ravn

Library of Congress Cataloging-in-Publication Data

Coupe, Robert.
 Body basics / by Robert Coupe.
     pages cm. — (Discovery education: how it works)
 Includes index.
 ISBN 978-1-4777-6309-4 (library binding) — ISBN 978-1-4777-6310-0 (pbk.) —
ISBN 978-1-4777-6311-7 (6-pack)
 1. Human body—Juvenile literature. 2. Human physiology—Juvenile literature. 3. Human anatomy—Juvenile literature. I. Title.
 QP37.C86 2014
 612—dc23
                    2013023120

Manufactured in the United States of America

CPSIA Compliance Information: Batch #W14PK2: For Further Information contact Rosen Publishing, New York, New York at 1-800-237-9932

HOW IT WORKS

BODY BASICS

ROBERT COUPE

PowerKiDS press

New York

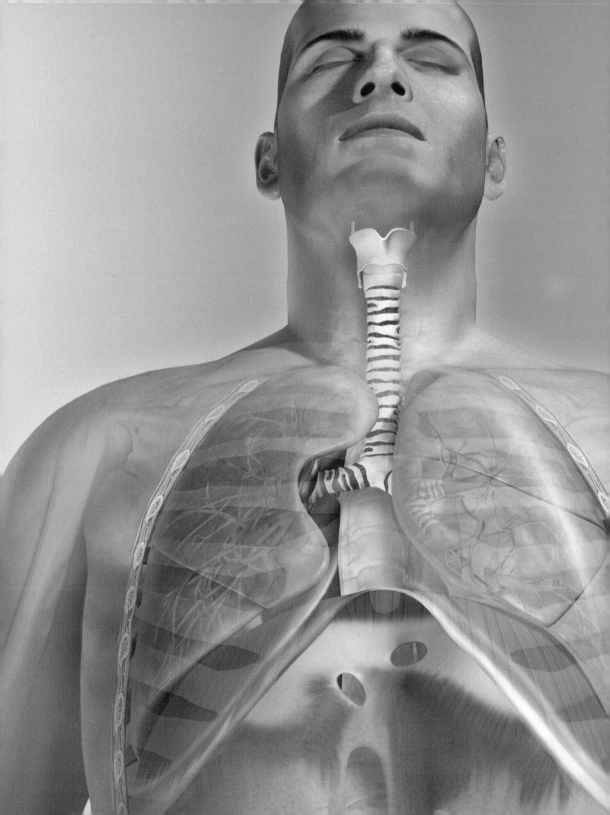

Contents

Body Building Blocks

Every living thing is made up of cells. Cells are the smallest parts of all plants, animals, and human beings. The human body contains about 100 million separate cells, which are like tiny factories that never stop working. There are about 200 different kinds of cells in the body. Each kind has its own job to do, but they all work together to keep the whole body healthy and energetic.

DNA
Short for deoxyribonucleic acid, DNA is in the center of every cell. It controls how the cell forms and works.

DIFFERENT CELLS

Different kinds of cells have very different shapes and sizes. Each kind of cell controls how a particular part of the body works.

Smooth muscle cells
These cells allow muscles in organs to move.

White blood cells
These cells in the blood help to fight against germs.

Nerve cells
These control how people react to feelings, such as pain, cold, and heat.

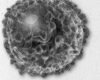

Sperm cells
These cells work to create baby humans and animals.

X and Y chromosomes
Chromosomes are part of a cell's DNA and control whether a body is male or female. Cells in female bodies have two chromosomes shaped like an X. Cells in male bodies have one X chromosome and one Y chromosome.

That's Amazing!
Old cells die and new ones replace them all the time. Every minute, more than 50 million cells in your body die and are replaced by new ones.

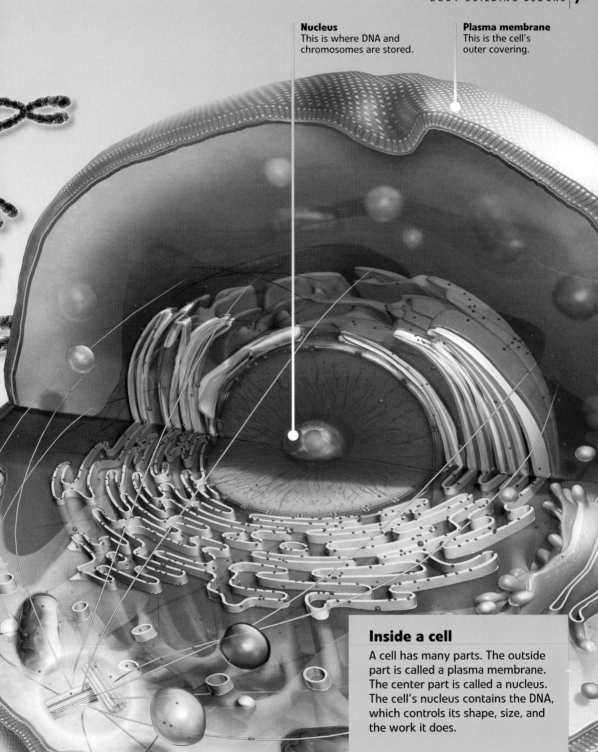

Nucleus
This is where DNA and
chromosomes are stored.

Plasma membrane
This is the cell's
outer covering.

Inside a cell

A cell has many parts. The outside
part is called a plasma membrane.
The center part is called a nucleus.
The cell's nucleus contains the DNA,
which controls its shape, size, and
the work it does.

Bones and Joints

Bones are strong and hard. All the bones in a person or animal make up their body's skeleton. Without bones to support it, your body would be soft and floppy, and you would not be able to stand, sit up, or move around. The size and position of different bones give a body its particular shape.

JOINTS

Bones do not bend, but joints in between allow bones to move up and down and from side to side. Different kinds of joints move in different ways.

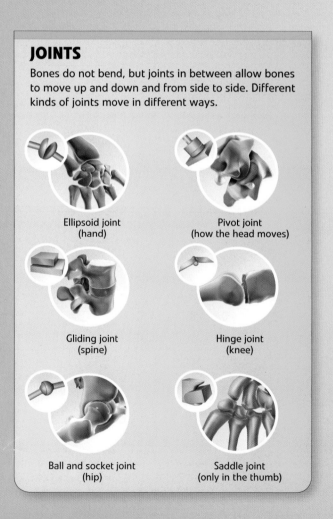

Ellipsoid joint
(hand)

Pivot joint
(how the head moves)

Gliding joint
(spine)

Hinge joint
(knee)

Ball and socket joint
(hip)

Saddle joint
(only in the thumb)

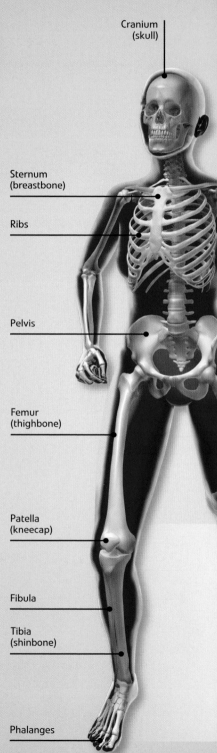

Cranium
(skull)

Sternum
(breastbone)

Ribs

Pelvis

Femur
(thighbone)

Patella
(kneecap)

Fibula

Tibia
(shinbone)

Phalanges

Skull

There are 22 bones in a human face and skull. Together, these bones protect the brain and give the face its shape.

Parietal bone

Frontal bone

Nasal bones

Temporal bone

Zygomatic bone (cheekbone)

Maxilla (upper jawbone)

Skeleton

A newborn baby has more than 300 bones, but as he or she grows, some bones join together. An adult human has just over 200 bones. They are many different shapes and sizes, and they all have particular jobs to do.

Mandible (lower jawbone)

Muscle Power

Every time a part of our body moves, it uses muscles. Muscles allow us to run, walk, jump, blink, talk, and sing. They also help us to eat and digest food. Many muscles inside our body work by themselves, and we cannot control them. The muscles that we can control are attached to our bones. These are called skeletal muscles.

Pulling up and pulling down

Some muscles in our face pull upward. They are called levators. Other muscles pull downward, and these are called depressors.

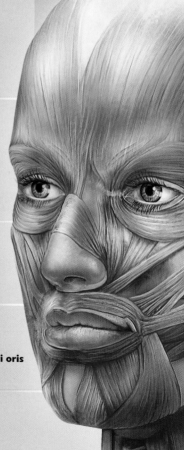

MAKING FACES

There are more than 50 muscles in our face. These stretch out or pull back like elastic bands when we smile, frown, or make other facial expressions.

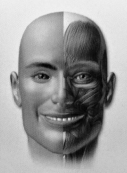

Smiling
This expression uses 12 facial muscles, and pulls the lips upward.

Frowning
This uses only 11 muscles. It pulls the lips down and causes the brow to become tight.

Frontalis
Pulls down when frowning.

Nasalis
Pulls down the tip of the nose.

Orbicularis oris
Controls lip during speech.

Depressor anguli oris
Pulls mouth out and down.

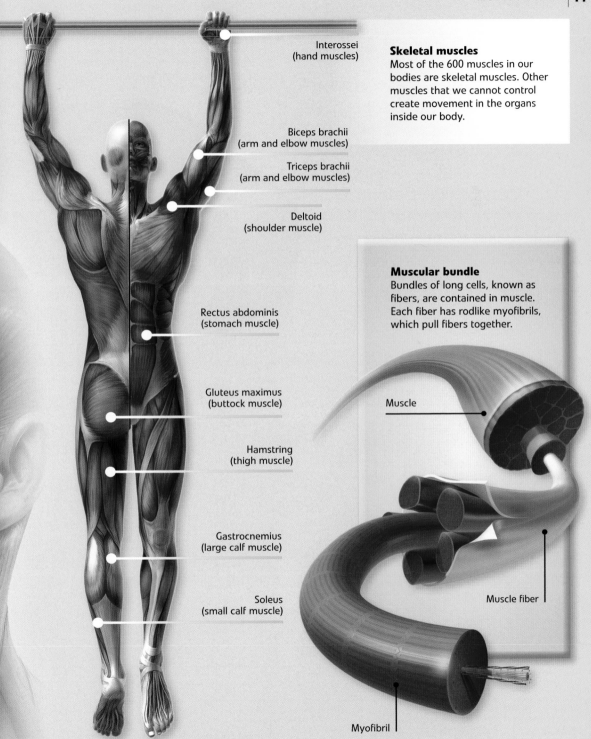

Interossei
(hand muscles)

Biceps brachii
(arm and elbow muscles)

Triceps brachii
(arm and elbow muscles)

Deltoid
(shoulder muscle)

Rectus abdominis
(stomach muscle)

Gluteus maximus
(buttock muscle)

Hamstring
(thigh muscle)

Gastrocnemius
(large calf muscle)

Soleus
(small calf muscle)

Skeletal muscles

Most of the 600 muscles in our bodies are skeletal muscles. Other muscles that we cannot control create movement in the organs inside our body.

Muscular bundle

Bundles of long cells, known as fibers, are contained in muscle. Each fiber has rodlike myofibrils, which pull fibers together.

Muscle

Muscle fiber

Myofibril

Circulation

When we breathe in, a gas called oxygen enters our lungs. From there it goes into our blood, then our heart pumps it through tubes, called blood vessels, to every part of our body. Our cells need oxygen to keep working and stay healthy. The moving blood also helps to keep our body at the right temperature. It also carries white blood cells that help fight disease.

Arteries
The large tubes that carry blood away from the heart and to distant parts of the body are called arteries. They have thick, muscular walls.

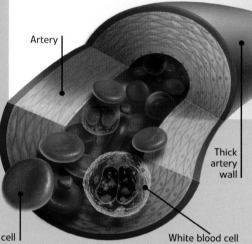

Artery

Thick artery wall

Red blood cell

White blood cell

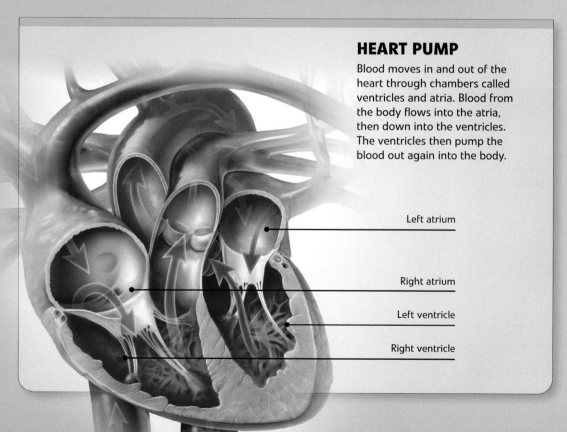

HEART PUMP

Blood moves in and out of the heart through chambers called ventricles and atria. Blood from the body flows into the atria, then down into the ventricles. The ventricles then pump the blood out again into the body.

Left atrium

Right atrium

Left ventricle

Right ventricle

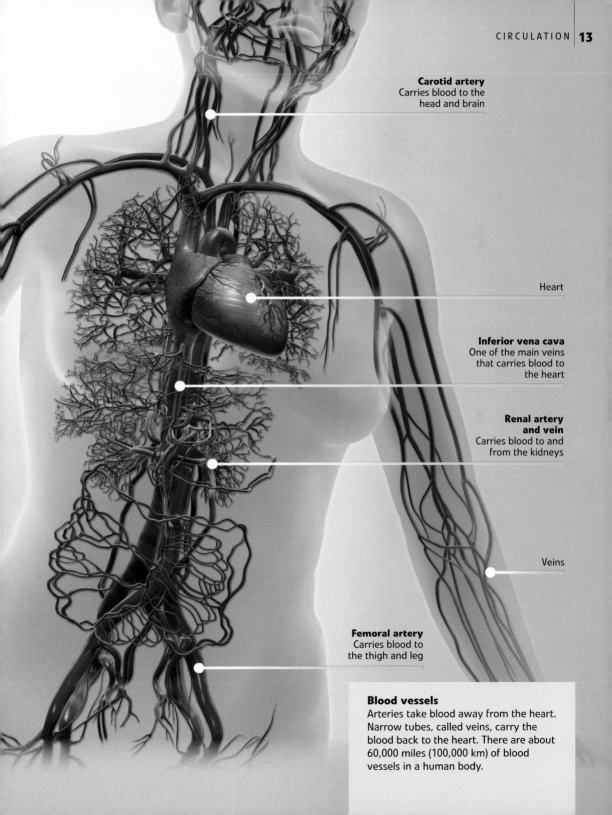

Carotid artery
Carries blood to the
head and brain

Heart

Inferior vena cava
One of the main veins
that carries blood to
the heart

**Renal artery
and vein**
Carries blood to and
from the kidneys

Veins

Femoral artery
Carries blood to
the thigh and leg

Blood vessels
Arteries take blood away from the heart.
Narrow tubes, called veins, carry the
blood back to the heart. There are about
60,000 miles (100,000 km) of blood
vessels in a human body.

Breath of Life

Breathing is so natural that we do it without thinking. We need to breathe all the time to stay alive. We breathe in to get the oxygen that our body needs. We breathe out to get rid of carbon dioxide. When we breathe in, we draw air into our lungs. Oxygen from this air then passes into our blood. Next, our heart pumps the blood all through our body.

Trachea, or windpipe
Air breathed in goes down the trachea to the lungs.

Bronchus
This is the large tube in each lung that brings in air from the trachea.

Right lung

BREATHING MUSCLE

The diaphragm is our breathing muscle. When we breathe in, our diaphragm tightens and stretches our lungs down and forward. When we breathe out, our diaphragm springs upward and pushes air out of our lungs.

Nasal cavity

Windpipe

Lungs

Diaphragm

Breathing in   **Breathing out**

Nose

Mouth

Bronchioles
These are the smallest
air tubes in the lungs.

Left lung

Tiny air pockets
Each lung contains about 300 million tiny air
pockets, called alveoli. Oxygen in the alveoli
is replaced by carbon dioxide.

Blood vessels
surround
alveoli.

Carbon dioxide
enters an
alveolus from
the blood.

Oxygen flows out of an
alveolus into the blood.

Lungs

The lungs are spongy organs in the chest.
Each lung has a large air tube, called a
bronchus, and millions of smaller air tubes,
called bronchioles.

Food for Energy and Growth

We need food for energy and to keep our body working. The food we eat travels first to our stomach, where it is churned up into a creamy liquid. It then moves into long tubes, called intestines. From here, water and nutrients are absorbed into the bloodstream. What is left moves to the rectum, where it stays until it comes out of the body as feces.

SMALL AND LARGE

Food from the stomach travels into the small intestine, and from there into the large intestine. The small intestine is much narrower than the arge intestine, but it is four times as long.

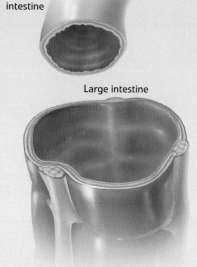

Small intestine

Large intestine

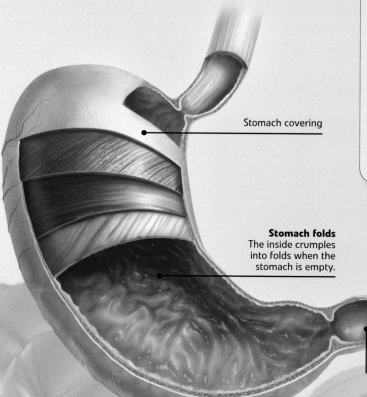

Stomach covering

Stomach folds
The inside crumples into folds when the stomach is empty.

Food processor
The stomach is like a bag with sides that can move in and out. It uses strong, squeezing actions to break up food.

Start of the intestines

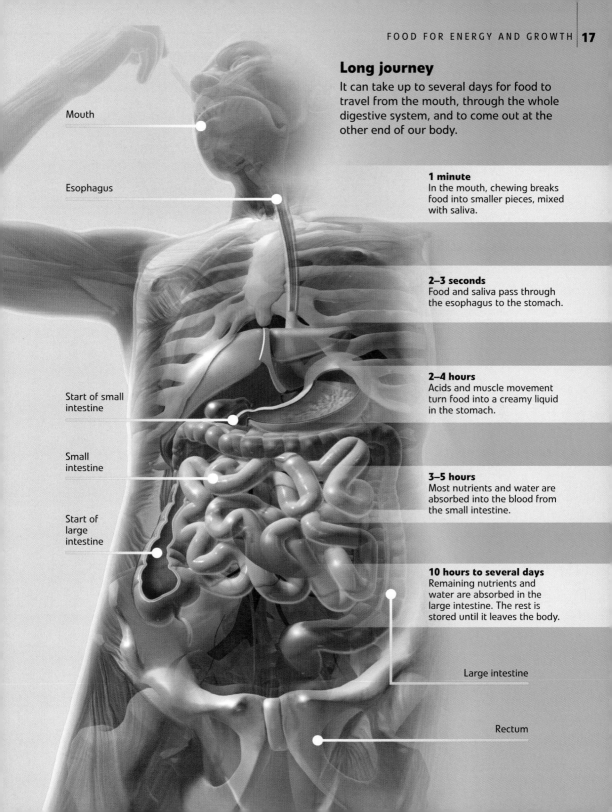

Mouth

Esophagus

Long journey

It can take up to several days for food to travel from the mouth, through the whole digestive system, and to come out at the other end of our body.

1 minute
In the mouth, chewing breaks food into smaller pieces, mixed with saliva.

2–3 seconds
Food and saliva pass through the esophagus to the stomach.

Start of small intestine

2–4 hours
Acids and muscle movement turn food into a creamy liquid in the stomach.

Small intestine

3–5 hours
Most nutrients and water are absorbed into the blood from the small intestine.

Start of large intestine

10 hours to several days
Remaining nutrients and water are absorbed in the large intestine. The rest is stored until it leaves the body.

Large intestine

Rectum

Attack and Defense

Skin and hair provide barriers against germs and harmful bacteria that could get into our body and cause illness. If germs do reach our bloodstream, the body has other defenses. White blood cells are powerful defenders against germs and harmful bacteria. They are an important part of our body's immune system.

White blood cells
Most blood cells are red. The white blood cells, although fewer in number, are the ones that protect us from sicknesses.

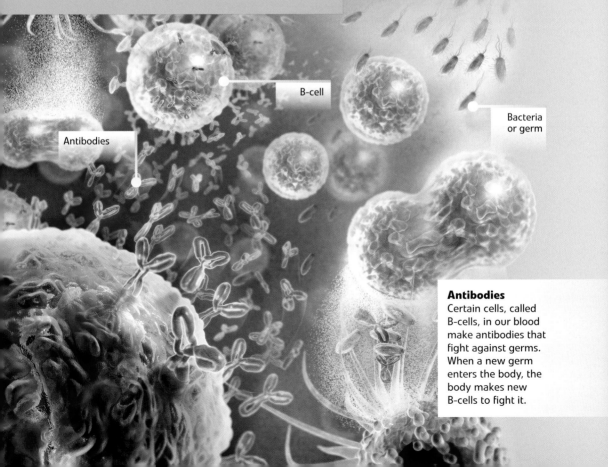

B-cell

Bacteria or germ

Antibodies

Antibodies
Certain cells, called B-cells, in our blood make antibodies that fight against germs. When a new germ enters the body, the body makes new B-cells to fight it.

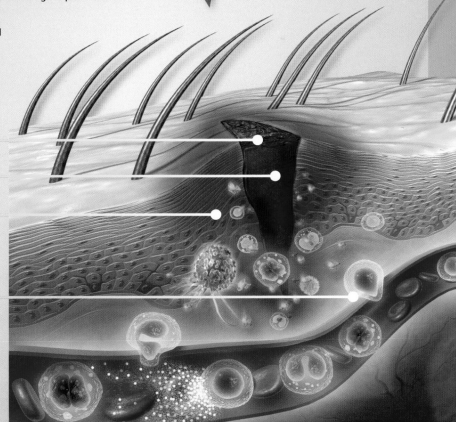

Dealing with injury

The skin is the body's first defense. If the skin is cut or bruised, the body's immune system springs swiftly into action to heal the wound. Blood vessels rush white blood cells to where the injury is. They trap and destroy germs.

Germs enter bloodstream.

Hair

Broken glass pierces skin.

Blood vessel

Scab forms on top of wound.

Blood clot forms.

Inflamed area near injury

White blood cells

Control Center

The brain is the control room for all of the body. It controls what we see, hear, taste, smell, and feel. It tells us when we are hungry, thirsty, tired, or in pain. It allows us to think, dream, remember, and work. Nerves carry messages from the brain to all parts of the body.

Corpus callosum
This area links the two hemispheres of the brain.

Right hemisphere
This half of the cerebrum controls movement in the left side of the body.

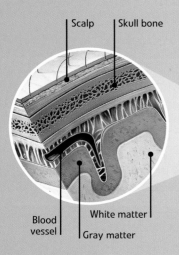

Scalp Skull bone

Blood vessel White matter Gray matter

Cerebellum
This helps to control balance and muscle movement.

Protection
The brain consists of two types of material called gray matter and white matter. Gray matter is the outer part of the brain. This gray matter is soft and folded over in thick layers.

Spinal cord
This goes down the back of the body and carries nerve signals to and from the brain.

Parts of the brain

There are three main parts of the brain. The cerebrum is the largest part. It consists of two parts—the left and right hemispheres. The cerebellum controls movement and the brain stem controls breathing and other things we do automatically.

Thalamus
This directs signals into and out of the brain.

Hippocampus
This controls memory, feelings, and emotions.

Medulla oblongata
This part of the brain stem controls movements that happen automatically in the body.

Facial nerve
This controls movement of many muscles in the face.

Brain stem
This connects the brain with the spinal cord, linking the brain with the rest of the body.

MESSAGE LINES

These yellow lines show the thin, wirelike fibers, called nerves, along which messages travel away from and back to the spinal cord. Some nerves act in groups to send messages to and receive them from particular areas of the body.

Brain

Spinal cord

Lumbar plexus

Sacral plexus

Neurons

Every nerve is made up of thousands of nerve cells, called neurons. Messages travel along the neuron's arm, or axon, and across gaps, called synapses, between cells. Dendrites then pass the messages farther on.

Axon

The Nervous System

Messages are constantly moving between our brain and our body. These messages travel from the brain stem to the spinal cord. From here, lines of nerves, like wires, carry them to all the other parts of the body, and then back again. Together, the brain, nerves, and spinal cord make up what we call our nervous system.

That's Amazing!

Neurons can carry messages along nerves and through our whole body at a speed of 300 feet (90 m) per second.

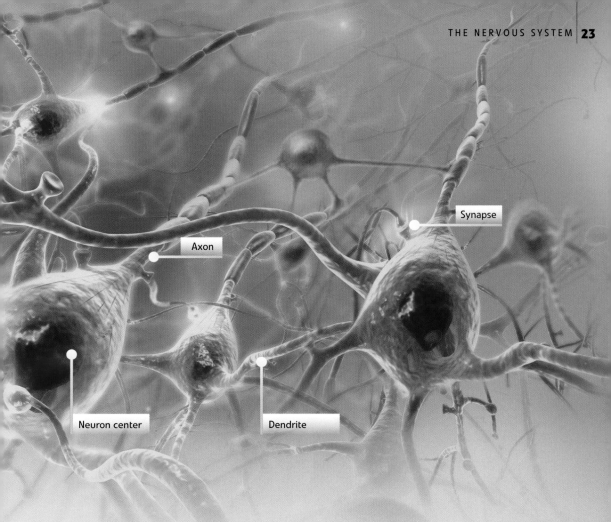

Synapse

Axon

Neuron center

Dendrite

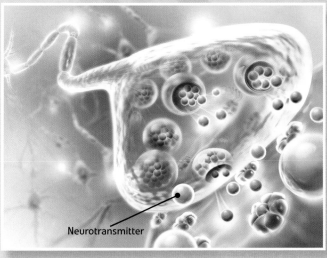

Neurotransmitter

A neuron in action
A neuron remains still until a message from the brain reaches it. Then, parts of the neuron, called neurotransmitters, spring into action. They pass the message through the cell and across the synapse to the next neuron.

Senses

Our body has five basic senses. We use them to see, smell, hear, feel, and taste things that we come into contact with. We rely on all five senses in our everyday life. Sight and hearing are probably the senses we rely on most to understand the world around us.

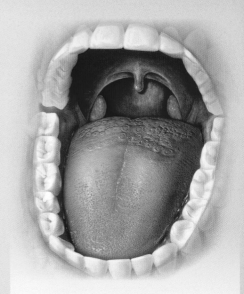

Taste
On the top of the tongue are more than 8,000 taste buds. The brain separates out four main kinds of tastes: salty, bitter, sour, and sweet.

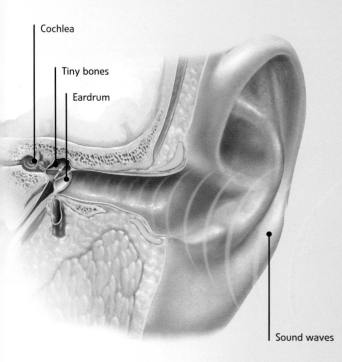

Cochlea

Tiny bones

Eardrum

Sound waves

Hearing
Sound waves in the air bounce off the eardrum. Bones behind it vibrate and send waves into the cochlea, where nerves send sound messages to the brain.

Nerve endings

Touch
When you touch something, nerve endings in your skin tell you whether it is hot or cold, rough or smooth, or painful or pleasant.

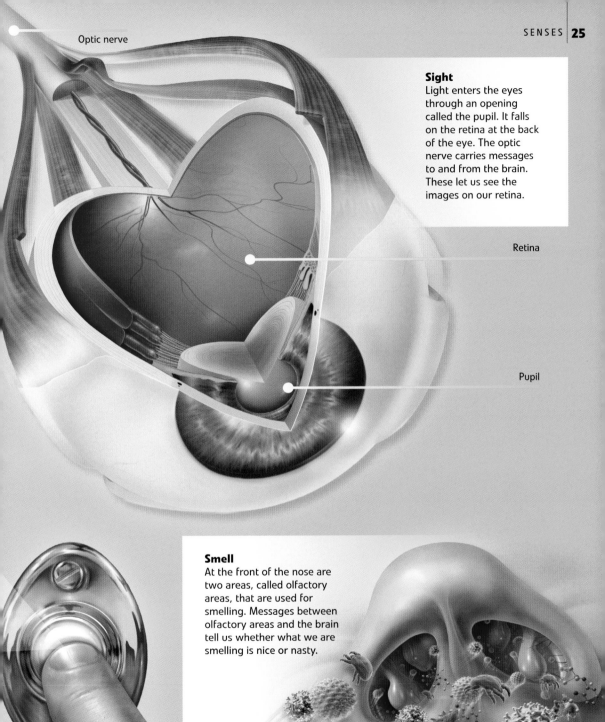

Optic nerve

Retina

Pupil

Sight

Light enters the eyes through an opening called the pupil. It falls on the retina at the back of the eye. The optic nerve carries messages to and from the brain. These let us see the images on our retina.

Smell

At the front of the nose are two areas, called olfactory areas, that are used for smelling. Messages between olfactory areas and the brain tell us whether what we are smelling is nice or nasty.

Birth and Growth

Human babies, like the babies of other mammals, grow and develop inside their mother's womb before they are born. Humans grow in the womb for about 9 months. A newborn baby slowly learns how to crawl, walk, and talk. It then continues its journey through life.

Two weeks
The embryo is a disk surrounded by a yolk sac.

Four weeks
The heart is beating and is pumping blood.

Six weeks
The embryo has grown longer, and eyes and ears begin to develop.

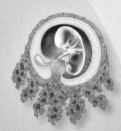

Eight weeks
The major organs are developing. The umbilical cord connects the embryo to the mother's bloodstream.

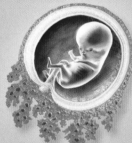

Twelve weeks
By this stage the embryo is called a fetus. It is now almost 2.5 inches (6 cm) long.

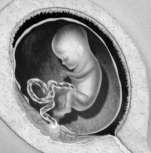

38 weeks
The fetus's organs are now working. The baby is ready to be born.

Growing in the womb

A baby begins as a tiny embryo. Over the months ahead, its organs and limbs develop, as it turns into a fully grown baby.

Toddler

A three-year-old child has very smooth, soft skin. At this stage, most children enjoy making new friends.

Aging

Children grow most rapidly in their first two years of life. In this period, they learn to walk and talk, and develop many other skills.

Learning new skills

By the time a child is five years old, he or she has learned to draw and perhaps read and write simple words.

Toward adulthood

Teenagers' bodies change in important ways as they become adults. They think for themselves and become more responsible.

Grown up

By the time a person is 20, they have grown as tall as they will ever be. They are now an adult.

80 years old

As people age, their skin becomes wrinkled. They also become weaker as they lose muscle cells.

Through the Ages

Over time, people have gradually learned more about the human body and how it works. They have also learned about diseases and worked out better ways to prevent and cure them.

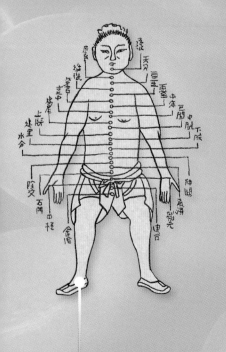

Ancient times
More than 5,000 years ago, splints were used for treating bone fractures. In China, acupuncture was used for healing.

Greek and Roman times
In ancient Greece, Hippocrates was one of the first people to study the body in detail.

Arabic medicine
About 1,000 years ago, Arab people used herbs and flowers as medicine. They also started to operate on sick people.

Middle Ages
Leeches were used to try to suck diseases out of bodies. People also believed that magic could cure illnesses.

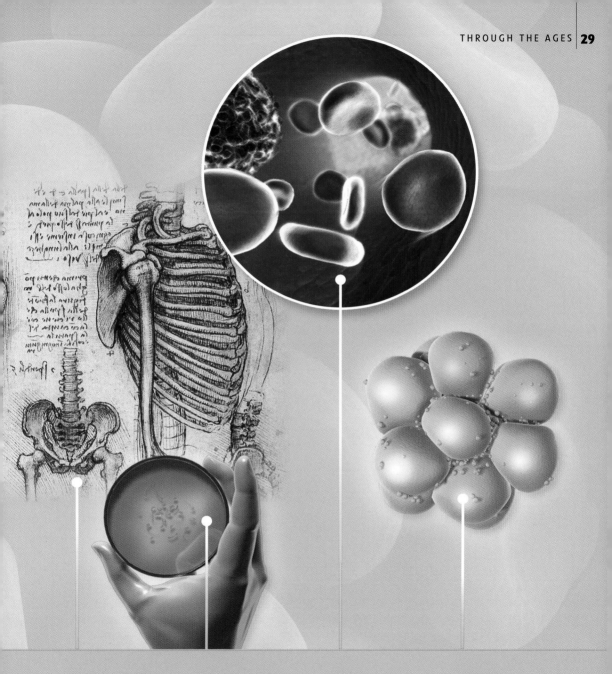

The Renaissance
By 1500, more was understood about the body. Leonardo da Vinci, an Italian, made detailed drawings of the body.

1700s and 1800s
Vaccinations were used to prevent diseases. Germs were discovered to be the cause of infections and illnesses.

1900s
Antibiotics were used to destroy many infections. Organ transplants and blood transfusions started to be performed.

2000s
Scientists are researching the use of specialized human cells, called stem cells, for treating cancer and many other diseases.

Mix and Match

Can you match the words on the right
to the descriptions on the left?

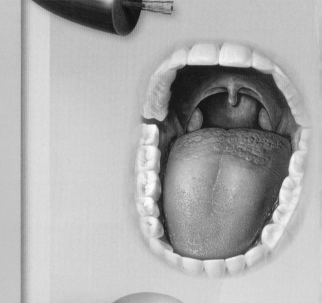

A

1 Where light comes
into your eye

2 Light falls here at
the back of your eye

3 The parts of a skeleton

4 Right and left sides
of your brains are
called these

5 Another word
for kneecap

6 Blood vessels that
bring blood to the heart

7 Our bodies need these
in order to move

8 Areas at the front of
your nose are called this

9 Where food from
your stomach goes

10 Two of your senses

B

muscles

hemispheres

olfactory

intestines

bones

retina

touch and hearing

veins

pupil

patella

Answers: 1 pupil **2** retina **3** bones **4** hemispheres **5** patella
6 veins **7** muscles **8** olfactory **9** intestines **10** touch and hearing

Glossary

alveoli (al-VEE-uh-ly)
Tiny air sacs in the lungs. Oxygen that is breathed in passes from the alveoli into the bloodstream.

arteries (AR-tu-reez)
Large blood vessels that carry blood away from the heart to other parts of the body.

atrium (AY-tree-um)
One of the two upper parts of the heart. Blood from the body flows into these.

bacteria (bak-TEER-ee-uh)
A group of tiny living things that have only a single cell. Some bacteria are useful to our bodies, while others are harmful and can cause disease.

carbon dioxide (KAR-bun dy-OK-syd)
A gas that we breathe out of our bodies.

chromosome (KROH-muh-sohm)
A tiny part of each cell in a plant or animal body. The kind of chromosomes in each cell decide what sex a body will be.

cochlea (KO-klee-uh)
Part of the inner ear. Nerves carry sound signals from the cochlea to the brain.

DNA (DEE EN AY)
A chemical in each cell in the body that makes up the cell's chromosomes.

eardrum (EER-drum)
A piece of tight skin in the ear that vibrates when sound waves strike it.

embryo (EM-bree-oh)
A very young infant that is forming inside its mother's womb.

fetus (FEE-tus)
An infant inside its mother's womb that is larger and more advanced than an embryo.

intestines (in-TES-tinz)
Long, winding tubes in the body. Food passes through them after it leaves the stomach.

joints (JOYNTS)
The places where bones connect to each other. Joints allow bones to move up and down and from side to side.

oxygen (OK-sih-jen)
A gas the body breathes in. Blood carries oxygen to every part of the body.

plasma (PLAZ-muh)
A substance that makes up just over half of a body's blood. Plasma is mainly water.

pupil (PYOO-pul)
A part of the eye. Light passes through the pupil and forms images on the retina.

retina (RET-in-uh)
The back part of the eyeball. Light and images that pass through the pupil fall on the retina.

synapse (SIH-naps)
A gap between nerve cells that are next to each other.

veins (VAYNZ)
Blood vessels that carry blood from all parts of the body toward the heart.

ventricle (VEN-trih-kul)
One of the two lower parts of the heart. The heart pumps blood out of the ventricles.

Index

A

adults 27
arteries 12, 13

B

bacteria 18
blood 6, 12, 13, 14, 15, 17,
  18, 20, 26, 30
bones 8, 9, 10, 20, 24, 30
brain 9, 13, 20, 21, 22, 23,
  24, 25
brain stem 21, 22

C

carbon dioxide 14, 15
cells 6, 7, 11, 12, 18, 19, 22,
  23, 29
children 27
chromosomes 6, 7

D

diaphragm 14
digestion 10, 17
diseases 12, 28, 29
DNA 6, 7

E

ear 24, 26
eye 25, 26, 30

F

fetus 26
food 10, 16, 17, 30

G

germs 18, 16, 19, 29

H

hair 18, 19
hearing 24, 30
heart 12, 13, 14, 26, 30
Hippocrates 28

I

immune system 18, 19
intestines 16, 17, 30

L

Leonardo da Vinci 29
lungs 12, 14, 15

M

muscles 6, 10, 11, 14, 17,
  21, 30

N

nerves 20, 21, 22, 23, 24, 25
nervous system 22, 23
neurons 22, 23

O

oxygen 12, 14, 15

P

pupil 25, 30

R

retina 25, 30

S

senses 24, 25
sight 24, 25
skeletal muscles 10, 11
skeleton 8, 9, 30
skin 18, 19, 24, 27
skull 8, 9
smell 25
spinal cord 20, 21, 22
stomach 16, 17, 30

T

taste 24
tongue 24
touch 24, 30

V

veins 13, 30

Websites

Due to the changing nature of Internet links, PowerKids Press has developed an online list of websites related to the subject of this book. This site is updated regularly. Please use this link to access the list:

www.powerkidslinks.com/disc/body/